AI-Powered C ....g

Top Tools for Software Development in 2024

Emma Royce Smartley

DEDICATION

This book is dedicated to all of the innovators, creators, and problem solvers in the field of software development. We are all inspired by your unwavering dedication to pushing technological frontiers and your unwavering pursuit of perfection. I hope that this book will be a useful tool for you as you go, enabling you to use AI to improve your skills and influence the direction that coding takes.

DISCLAIMER

AI-Powered Coding: Top Tools for Software Development in 2024 contains content that is intended solely for informational and educational reasons. The writers and publishers do not guarantee the content's correctness, dependability, or suitability for any specific purpose, even though every effort has been taken to assure its accuracy and completeness.

Since the tools and technologies covered in this book are constantly changing, the authors advise readers to do their own study and due diligence before acting upon any advice or utilizing any of the software tools.

If you use or are unable to use the material in this book, the writers and publishers will not be responsible for any direct, indirect, incidental, or consequential damages. You understand and agree to this disclaimer in its entirety by reading this book.

CONTENTS

ACKNOWLEDGMENTS

To everyone who helped create *AI-Powered Coding: Top Tools for Software Development in 2024,* my sincere gratitude is extended.

I want to start by expressing my gratitude to my family and friends for their patience, support, and encouragement along this journey. Your confidence in me has always given me motivation.

My heartfelt gratitude goes out to all the specialists and developers whose knowledge and expertise helped to form the contents of this book. I, along with many others, am inspired by your commitment to innovation in the field of software development.

We especially appreciate the reviews and beta readers who helped us polish and improve the chapters with their insightful comments. Your constructive critique and excitement for the issue were important in bringing this book to life.

I also want to thank the innumerable developers and organizations whose contributions to software development using AI have made our work easier and more productive. Your inventiveness and dedication to the advancement of technology are admirable.

Lastly, I would like to thank my publisher and the whole publishing team for all of their help and advice in making this project a reality. This has been a wonderful and pleasurable experience thanks to your professionalism and skill.

I appreciate your participation in this adventure, everyone.

CHAPTER 1

OVERVIEW OF AI CODING INSTRUMENTS

In 2024, artificial intelligence (AI) is transforming the software development industry. AI coding tools have revolutionized the way we create, debug, and optimize code, making them essential tools for developers. The progress of AI in software development will be examined in this chapter, along with the definition and significance of AI coding helpers in the contemporary programming environment.

1.1 SOFTWARE DEVELOPMENT'S AI EVOLUTION

Over the past ten years, AI's place in software development has changed dramatically. Software development is now more intelligent, scalable, and efficient thanks to the incorporation of AI technologies, which range from simple automation to sophisticated AI-driven coding assistants.

Initial Automation:

Automation techniques streamlined monotonous processes like code formatting and syntax checking early in the software development cycle. These technologies, however helpful, were restricted to rule-based systems that needed developers to provide specific instructions. They could neither "learn" nor "reason" about code, and they provided little help other than surface-level automation.

Innovations in Machine Learning:

A revolutionary development in coding tools was the use of machine learning (ML) techniques. Large-scale source code analyses allowed machine learning models to recognize programming trends, grow from prior errors, and make recommendations that went beyond simple automation. One of the early applications of machine learning (ML) was in code autocompletion systems such as TabNine, which offer context-aware code suggestions based on real-time analysis of the developer's work.

Natural Language Processing (NLP) in the Context of Coding:

Lately, NLP has made it possible for AI systems to translate machine code into human language. Tools that are able to create complete code blocks from natural language descriptions have been made possible by the advent of large language models such as GPT (Generative Pre-trained Transformer). Developers can now describe a function in simple English, and an AI coding tool can generate the matching code, decreasing the cognitive burden and physical labor necessary in the development process.

2024: The Age of AI-Enhanced Coding Tools:

AI coding helpers are more advanced than ever in 2024. They give code security insights, refactoring recommendations, intelligent bug identification, and performance optimization in addition to autocompletion assistance. Developers are now able to create more dependable, maintainable, and scalable solutions in addition to writing code more quickly thanks to the next generation of AI technologies.

1.2 WHAT IS AN AI CODING HELPER?

AI coding assistants are specialized software tools meant to help developers at every stage of the software development lifecycle. They are driven by AI and ML algorithms. They offer a range of functionalities that streamline various operations, enabling developers to focus more on high-level problem-solving rather than repetitive, low-level coding effort. Here is a summary of their salient characteristics:

Autocompletion of Code:

Intelligent suggestions to finish lines of code are provided by AI-driven auto completion tools, such as GitHub Copilot, which examine the context of the code you're writing. Their comprehension of variable names, functions, and code structures aids in decreasing errors and speeding up the coding process.

Error prediction and bug detection:

AI coding helpers are able to foresee problems or defects in the code while it is being written. These tools can identify error-prone sections and recommend corrections even before the code is built or executed, by examining coding patterns and consulting extensive databases of past defects.

Generation of Code:

High-level requirements or natural language input can be fed into advanced AI technologies, which can then produce functional code. For instance, the AI tool will provide an efficient and useful code block for the developer if they enter, "Create a Python function to calculate the factorial of a number." This feature considerably accelerates the prototype phase.

Refactoring Code:

The practice of refactoring and improving the structure of

existing code without changing its behavior—may be suggested by AI coding assistants, and they can even automate it. Through a grasp of the architecture of the code, these tools help improve its efficiency, readability, and maintainability.

Vulnerability detection and security insights:

Developers can repair security weaknesses during development rather than after release by using AI-powered tools to check code for vulnerabilities. These programs have the ability to offer suggestions based on security database known attacks and recommended practices.

Incorporation into Development Settings:

Integrated Development Environments (IDEs) such as Visual Studio Code, JetBrains IntelliJ, or web-based platforms like GitHub are commonly used to incorporate AI coding assistance. The tools are pleasant and simple to use because of this seamless integration, which guarantees that they are available directly within the developer's workflow.

1.3 AI's Significance in Contemporary Software Development

Artificial intelligence (AI) coding tools are being used more and more due to the complexity of software applications increasing, the need for more trustworthy code, and the demand to deliver faster. These tools are becoming vital parts of contemporary development processes, not only "nice-to-have" extras. AI is essential in today's software development ecosystem for the following reasons:

Increasing Productivity of Developers:

Artificial intelligence (AI) coding tools greatly increase productivity by generating smart recommendations and automating repetitive operations. Jobs that used to take hours, such troubleshooting, finding code snippets, and refactoring, can now be completed in a matter of minutes. Because of their enhanced productivity, developers are able to devote more time to the strategic and artistic parts of coding, such as creating system structures and algorithms.

Improving the Caliber of Code:

AI-powered solutions for code analysis and bug finding help to lower human error and enhance the quality of the code. AI tools stop expensive bugs from entering production because they may identify possible problems early in the development process. Continuous code monitoring using AI makes sure the codebase is stable, safe, and expandable.

Speeding Up the Development Process:

Speed is essential in the continuous integration/continuous delivery (CI/CD) and agile development age. The entire development lifecycle—from basic code creation to testing and deployment—is accelerated by AI coding tools. Artificial Intelligence (AI) helps developers to achieve deadlines without sacrificing code quality by automating repetitive coding processes and offering real-time assistance.

Minimizing Developers' Cognitive Stress:

Programming is a mentally taxing task that needs acute concentration and meticulous attention to detail. AI coding assistants offer code explanations, context-aware suggestions, and autocomplete features to help reduce some of the cognitive load. This makes it easier for developers to work, which lessens tiredness and lowers the possibility of mistakes.

Improving Cooperation and Information Exchange:

By offering standardized code recommendations, AI solutions can help in collaborative development environments and ensure uniformity among teams. By describing code snippets and offering best practices, they can also aid in the education of junior developers. AI-driven insights gradually help level the playing field between more and less experienced developers, creating an atmosphere that is more inclusive and productive.

Facilitating Innovation:

Developers now have more time for innovation as AI handles monotonous coding duties. They can concentrate on developing new features, investigating cutting-edge technology, and resolving challenging issues that AI is still unable to manage. AI coding tools allow developers to push the limits of what's possible in software development, enhancing human creativity rather than replacing it.

AI coding tools in 2024 will be far more than just helpers; they will be essential to contemporary software development methods. Through task automation, issue detection, and productivity boosts, they enable engineers to generate better code more quickly. Any developer hoping to stay competitive in a quickly changing technical landscape has to understand these technologies.

CHAPTER 2

TOOLS FOR CODING COMPLETION

Code completion tools have become indispensable resources in the ever-changing world of software development, helping to improve both productivity and code quality. With real-time code suggestions, speedier coding, and a lower chance of errors, these AI-powered assistants support developers. This chapter explores the features, benefits, and ways that three popular code completion tools GitHub Copilot, Amazon CodeWhisperer, and Codeium adjust development processes more effectively.

2.1 THE AI PAIR PROGRAMMER, GITHUB COPILOT

GitHub and OpenAI worked together to build GitHub Copilot, an AI-powered code completion tool. It is intended to act as a sophisticated pair programmer, offering developers context-aware code recommendations based on comments and the current code context. Here are some details about its attributes and advantages:

Aware of Context Suggestions:

GitHub Copilot's ability to produce contextually relevant suggestions is one of its best features. Copilot provides real-time suggestions that are in line with the developer's goal by examining previously written code. To calculate a factorial, for example, a developer can start entering a function and Copilot will propose the entire code, including parameters and return statements, according to the programming language being used.

Multiple Language Support:

GitHub Numerous programming languages are supported by Copilot, such as Python, JavaScript, TypeScript, Ruby, Go, and others. Because of its adaptability, developers using a variety of tech stacks can benefit from Copilot's recommendations regardless of the language or framework they're using.

Integrated IDEs Seamlessly:

Popular integrated programming environments (IDEs)

including Visual Studio Code, JetBrains IDEs, and Neovim are easily integrated with Copilot. Through this interface, developers may utilize Copilot's recommendations straight from within their workflow, which expedites the coding process without interfering with their comfortable setting.

Growing from Feedback and Context:

Through ongoing learning from developer interactions, Copilot is able to improve its recommendations over time. Copilot adjusts to developers' coding tastes and styles when they accept, reject, or edit the offered code snippets, which makes it more and more efficient at providing pertinent ideas.

Increasing Productivity of Developers:

GitHub Copilot greatly increases developer productivity by cutting down on the amount of time spent creating boilerplate code, finding documentation, and debugging. Developers can concentrate on more complex design and problem-solving activities, which will speed up project completion and improve workflow.

2.2 Cloud-Native Code Generation with Amazon CodeWhisperer

A cloud-native code generating tool called Amazon CodeWhisperer is designed to make coding easier, especially for developers that interact with the Amazon Web Services (AWS) ecosystem. CodeWhisperer encourages best practices and increases productivity with its extensive feature set. Here's a closer look at what it can do:

The integration of AWS:

Because CodeWhisperer is seamlessly linked with AWS services, developers creating cloud-based applications will find it to be an excellent option. The program may automatically recommend short bits of code that make use of AWS SDKs, facilitating developers' quick and easy access to AWS services like Lambda, DynamoDB, and S3. Through the provision of pertinent code examples and best practices, this integration speeds up the creation of cloud-based apps.

Versatility in Language:

CodeWhisperer is compatible with several programming languages, such as Python, Java, JavaScript, C#, and more, much like GitHub Copilot. Because of this adaptability, developers may work efficiently on a variety of projects because they can obtain ideas that are appropriate regardless of the language that they prefer.

In-the-moment Suggestions:

Based on the project's context, CodeWhisperer offers real-time code recommendations. It may recommend whole code snippets, such as function declarations, API calls, and data manipulations, by examining the code that has already been produced. This real-time feedback reduces disruptions and aids developers in maintaining their work flow.

Features for Security and Compliance:

There are features in Amazon CodeWhisperer that support compliance and security. It can point up possible security holes in the code and make recommendations for changes to guarantee best practices are followed. Given the potential consequences of security lapses and data spills in the modern world, this competence is especially vital.

- **Collaboration is the Main Aim:** CodeWhisperer promotes cooperation between development teams by offering standardized code recommendations that are in line with corporate guidelines. The tool lessens the possibility of integration problems by promoting the use of standard coding techniques, which helps maintain code quality and coherence across team projects.

2.3 CODEIUM: COPILOT'S FREE SUBSTITUTE

Codeium markets itself as a cost-free substitute for GitHub Copilot and other high-end coding aids. With a number of characteristics that make it a desirable option for developers, Codeium aims to democratize access to AI-driven coding assistance. Below is a summary of its main features:

Economically Sound Option:

Codeium is free to use, in contrast to other coding aids that could charge a monthly subscription. Because of its accessibility, it's a desirable choice for startups, students, and independent developers looking to use AI technology without breaking the bank.

Completion of the Smart Code:

Like its premium competitors, Codeium offers intelligent code completion suggestions. It helps developers write code more precisely and efficiently by generating pertinent suggestions based on an analysis of the context of the present code.

Multilingual Compatibility:

Numerous programming languages, such as Python, JavaScript, TypeScript, Java, and others, are supported by Codeium. This wide-ranging language support ensures that developers working on varied projects may utilize the tool effectively.

Interface Friendly to Users:

Codeium's user-friendly interface, which was created with usability in mind, makes it simple for developers to browse through ideas and alter settings to suit their needs. Because of its simplicity, new users who might not be familiar with sophisticated coding tools are more likely to adopt it.

Learning and Community Resources:

Codeium creates a community around its technology by giving users access to tutorials, learning materials, and forums where they can exchange advice and best practices. The user experience is improved by this community-driven strategy, which also promotes cooperation and knowledge exchange.

Privacy and Data Security Are Emphasized:

Codeium lays a lot of focus on user data protection as developers grow more conscious of data privacy and security issues. Because the tool doesn't save or distribute user code snippets, developers may use it with confidence knowing that private data won't be compromised.

Code completion tools like Codeium, GitHub Copilot, and Amazon CodeWhisperer are crucial to contemporary software development. These solutions improve developer productivity, expedite the coding process, and advance code quality by utilizing AI technologies. These AI-driven tools will continue to lead the software development scene as the need for effective coding solutions grows, enabling developers to create reliable applications more quickly and easily.

CHAPTER 3

CODE GENERATION POWERED BY AI

The use of AI to generate code is revolutionizing the way developers approach writing code. With the use of machine learning and natural language processing, these tools let developers write code with never-before-seen ease or efficiency. We will look at three well-known AI-powered code generation tools in this chapter: ChatGPT, Claude by Anthropic, and Cody by Sourcegraph. Each tool brings distinct skills to the table, helping developers to write high-quality code and boost their overall productivity.

3.1 CHATGPT: CONVERTING NATURAL LANGUAGE INTO CODE

With the use of sophisticated natural language processing, OpenAI's ChatGPT makes it easier to generate code from descriptions in natural language. This feature makes coding much more efficient and makes the code more accessible to developers of all skill levels. This is a thorough examination of its attributes and capabilities:

Intelligent Language Perception:

The capacity of ChatGPT to understand and interpret input in natural language is fundamental to its functionality. Developers can use ChatGPT to produce code snippets that correlate to their plain English description of what they want the code to accomplish. This improves the intuitiveness of coding, especially for people who might not be familiar with particular programming languages.

Multiple Programming Language Support:

Python, JavaScript, Java, C++, Ruby, and other programming languages are just a few of the languages in which ChatGPT can generate code. Because of its adaptability, developers can use ChatGPT for a variety of applications, independent of the language or framework they prefer. For instance, without switching tools, a user can ask for a function in Python and then transition to asking for a comparable function in Java.

Best Practices and Code Structure:

ChatGPT can provide code, but it can also include best practices in its outputs. It can help developers produce cleaner, more maintainable code by making recommendations for appropriate naming conventions, code architectures, and optimization strategies when asked. This feature is very helpful for inexperienced developers who want to learn and get better at coding.

Active Coding Workshops:

Developers can propose changes to generated code, ask follow-up questions, and get clarifications during interactive coding sessions facilitated by ChatGPT. With the help of this conversational interface, developers can work together in a collaborative setting and improve their code iteratively in response to immediate feedback.

Restrictions and Moral Perspectives:

Even though ChatGPT is an effective tool, it's vital to understand its limitations. It's possible that the generated code isn't always flawlessly aligned with requirements or error-free. Code should be tested and reviewed by developers before being put into production settings. Furthermore, ethical issues pertaining to data security and privacy must be taken into mind, especially when handling sensitive data.

3.2 CLAUDE: CLARIFICATIONS AND AI-ASSISTED CODING

The Claude tool from Anthropic is a noteworthy development in AI-assisted coding because it can produce code and provide thorough explanations of it as well. This function is particularly beneficial for educational purposes and skill development. Here's a closer look at Claude's capabilities:

Generating Contextual Code:

Claude is built to comprehend the environment in which it functions. When a developer submits a natural language description, Claude generates code that aligns with the provided criteria. In order to generate results that are more pertinent to the current discussion, it might also take into account prior encounters.

In-depth Justifications:

Claude's ability to offer thorough explanations for the code it creates is one of its best qualities. Claude can deconstruct a code snippet and elucidate its logic, structure, and purpose by breaking each component separately. Because of this instructional feature, Claude is a great tool for students who want to know why certain coding decisions are made in addition to learning to code.

Promoting Optimal Techniques:

Claude highlights the importance of coding best practices by offering suggestions for enhancements or different methods inside its explanations. For instance, it may advocate utilizing more efficient methods or indicate any security issues in the code. This advice broadens the skill set of developers and encourages them to approach coding with greater thoughtfulness.

Collaborative Learning Environment: A collaborative learning environment is fostered by Claude's interactive interface. Developers have the ability to inquire about individual code segments, request alternative implementations, or seek clarification on ideas. This conversation encourages deeper learning and active participation, which helps novices feel less intimidated by coding.

Use Cases in Mentoring and Education:

Claude is especially well-suited for mentoring initiatives, coding boot camps, and educational environments. Claude can be used by teachers to design coding tasks, offer immediate feedback, and lead discussions about coding principles. This application helps students become more self-assured developers while also enhancing their educational experience.

3.3 CODY BY SOURCEGRAPH: AI SUPPORT AT THE CODEBASE LEVEL

Cody, created by Sourcegraph, takes a distinct approach to AI-powered code development by emphasizing support at the codebase level. With the help of this feature, developers can produce code that adheres to the general organization and standards of their current codebases. Here is a detailed examination of Cody's attributes:

Aware of the Code Context:

Cody functions at the codebase level, which means it can evaluate and understand the existing code within a project.

Cody creates code by looking at variables, functions, and class structures, and then blending that code flawlessly into the overall design. This contextual knowledge improves code consistency and lessens the possibility of integration problems.

Project-Consistent Code Generation:

One of Cody's key advantages is its ability to write code that complies to the precise rules and patterns set inside a project. Developers can submit requests for additional features or functionalities, and Cody will produce code that adheres to the current structure, naming conventions, and style. Teams who are working on big codebases where consistency is important will find this capability especially helpful.

Code Lookup and Exploration:

Cody can generate code and has powerful code search features. Within their codebase, developers can easily locate pertinent code snippets or examples that aid in their understanding of the organization and implementation of existing code. By increasing productivity and saving time, this feature frees up developers to concentrate on creating new features rather than troubleshooting problems.

Collaboration and Team Integration:

Cody facilitates smooth interaction with project management tools and version control systems, which encourages cooperation among development teams. Cody allows teams to evaluate and discuss modifications to the code, as well as make sure that the code generated complies with team standards. This cooperative strategy promotes a culture of shared knowledge and improves communication.

Enhancing the Onboarding Process:

Another useful tool for onboarding new devs is Cody. Cody helps new team members quickly become acclimated to the code structure and norms by offering them context-aware ideas and advice at the codebase level. Their productivity within the team increases and the learning curve is lowered thanks to this support.

Cutting-edge methods for producing high-quality code are being made possible by AI-powered code generation tools like ChatGPT, Claude, and Cody. These tools are completely changing the coding industry. These technologies support best practices in coding, increase developer productivity, and encourage learning and teamwork. The industry's future will be greatly influenced by the incorporation of AI into software development, as the need for effective coding solutions only grows.

CHAPTER 4

CODE SECURITY AND QUALITY

It is now crucial to ensure code quality and security in the modern software development environment. With the complexity of applications growing and cyber dangers increasing, developers must use cutting edge technologies that improve code quality and protect it from vulnerabilities. This chapter examines three key facets of code quality and security: the significance of AI-driven code optimization and refactoring, the function of GitHub Security Lab and Copilot in preventing vulnerabilities, and Snyk's AI-powered code security.

4.1 SNYK: CODE SECURITY POWERED BY AI

As a leading tool in the field of code security, Snyk provides developers with an integrated approach to find and fix security flaws at every stage of the development process. Snyk's capabilities extend beyond simple scanning; it is made to blend in with current development workflows and provide real-time feedback and fixes.

Workflow Integration with Development:

Developers may find vulnerabilities early in the development process because to Snyk's seamless integration with version control systems, CI/CD pipelines, and well-known development tools. Snyk makes sure that security considerations are not an afterthought but rather a part of the development culture by integrating security checks into the workflow.

Real-Time Vulnerability Detection:

Snyk regularly monitors code repositories using sophisticated algorithms. Snyk is a real-time code analysis tool that highlights vulnerabilities in real-time as developers create code. Developers are able to proactively address security concerns thanks to this quick feedback loop, which greatly lowers the risk of delivering risky code.

Automated Corrections and Cleaning:

Beyond identification, Snyk offers practical

recommendations for correction. Snyk provides automated remedies or advice on how to properly address a vulnerability when it is found. This functionality helps developers to keep security without compromising productivity, which is especially useful in situations where deadlines are tight.

Scanning and Dependency Management:

Numerous third-party libraries and dependencies are frequently used by modern apps, which can pose security problems. These dependencies are scanned thoroughly by Snyk, which also finds known vulnerabilities in the project's libraries. Developers can greatly improve the security posture of their applications by maintaining secure and up-to-date dependencies.

Compliance and Reporting:

Additionally, Snyk offers comprehensive reporting features that let teams evaluate their security posture over time. These reports, which provide insights into vulnerability trends and remediation efficacy, can assist firms in demonstrating compliance with industry norms and standards.

4.2 Copilot's Role and the GitHub Security Lab

GitHub's integration of technologies such as the GitHub Security Lab and Copilot is essential to the company's efforts to promote secure development techniques, for which it has become known as a leader. When combined, they provide a strong framework that can be used to find and fix common vulnerabilities in codebases.

Lab for GitHub Security:

A strong initiative to strengthen open-source software security is GitHub Security Lab. It gives developers access to a collection of instruments made to find weaknesses and recommend solutions. The lab works with security researchers to make sure that new dangers are dealt with right away.

Security Analysis Integration:

Developers can do static analysis directly on their code thanks to GitHub's integration of security analysis tools. This feature aids in the early detection of security issues by revealing possible weaknesses before they can be taken advantage of. Developers can make sure that new code complies with security standards by adding security checks into the pull request procedure.

Help from GitHub Copilot:

GitHub Copilot is an AI-powered coding helper that enhances security protocols by providing context-aware code recommendations that put security first. Copilot can identify potential vulnerabilities in real time and recommend secure coding methods to developers while they write code. This proactive strategy not only boosts productivity but also cultivates a security-first culture among developers.

Avoiding Typical Vulnerabilities:

By encouraging developers to follow safe coding standards, GitHub lowers the risk of common vulnerabilities like buffer overflows, SQL injection, and cross-site scripting (XSS). By providing developers with up-to-date security knowledge and best practices, GitHub encourages a culture of secure software development.

Involvement in the Community and Ongoing

Education:

Additionally, GitHub Security Lab places a strong emphasis on community involvement, inviting developers to take part in finding and fixing vulnerabilities. By encouraging a culture of continuous learning, this cooperative approach helps engineers stay up to date on the most recent security threats and mitigation techniques.

4.3 AI-POWERED CODE OPTIMIZATION AND REWORKING

Code maintainability and performance become important considerations in software development as applications grow. AI-driven tools that assist code rewriting and optimization play a crucial role in ensuring that codebases remain clean, efficient, and scalable.

Refactoring Suggestions That Are Automated:

AI-driven technologies can automatically suggest refactorings based on an analysis of codebases to find places for improvement. This feature makes it easier for developers to maintain and expand their code by improving its structure without changing its exterior behavior. AI tools may suggest, for example, combining redundant code, enhancing naming standards, or rearrangement of code to make it easier to read.

Performance Enhancement:

AI-driven technologies can examine code performance indicators and recommend optimizations in addition to structural changes. Through the identification of bottlenecks, inefficient algorithms, or needless computations, these technologies enable developers to improve the performance of applications. By concentrating on optimization, applications are able to grow efficiently and provide a smooth user experience.

Cutting Down on Technical Debt:

Reducing technical debt is one of the main advantages of AI-driven refactoring. Through proactive problem-solving, developers can avert the build-up of challenges that may impede their future endeavors. By doing this, the code becomes of higher quality and requires less time and money to make improvements in the future.

Context-Aware Refactoring:

Cutting-edge AI technologies use machine learning to

comprehend the context in which code runs. Their context-aware methodology allows them to offer customized recommendations that take into account the particular needs of a certain project. Developers can get better outcomes by coordinating refactoring efforts with project objectives.

Incorporation into Development Settings:

Numerous AI-driven refactoring solutions offer real-time suggestions to developers while they code, integrating smoothly with well-known IDEs. By minimizing disruptions to the development workflow, this integration pushes developers to adopt refactoring as a continuous process as opposed to a one-time endeavor.

Cooperation and Code Evaluation:

AI-powered refactoring tools that offer insights during code reviews also help to improve teamwork. Teams can use these tools to evaluate the quality of the code, make suggestions for enhancements, and make sure best practices are followed. This cooperative method improves the overall quality of the code and encourages knowledge exchange within the team.

Security and high-quality code are essential components of contemporary software development. Snyk, GitHub Security Lab, and AI-driven refactoring tools are examples of tools that enable developers to write secure, well-written code quickly. The use of AI technology in these domains will be essential to developing a culture of security and excellence among development teams as the software landscape changes.

CHAPTER 5

DESIGN-TO-CODE AI TOOLS

The advent of design-to-code AI technologies has completely changed the process of creating digital products, as there is an increasing need for quick development cycles and smooth communication between designers and developers. With the use of these technologies, designers may more effectively convert their imaginative thoughts into usable code, bridging the gap between the two disciplines. In-depth analyses of the features, capabilities, and contributions of three prominent design-to-code AI tools Visual Copilot, Uizard, and TeleportHQ are provided in this chapter.

5.1 VISUAL COPILOT: CODING TO FIGMA DESIGNS

An effective solution for automating the translation of Figma designs into code for well-known frameworks like React, Vue, and Angular is Visual Copilot. Visual Copilot improves efficiency and reduces errors by optimizing the handoff process between design and development.

Figma Integration Done Seamlessly:

With Visual Copilot's direct integration with Figma, designers can work in their favorite environment and export their designs to code with ease. By doing away with the necessity for human translations, this integration guarantees that the finished code faithfully captures the original design intent.

Generating Code for Various Frameworks:

The flexibility of Visual Copilot to create code for several frameworks is one of its best advantages. Visual Copilot offers customized code outputs for teams using React, Vue, or Angular, letting developers use the framework that best fits their project needs. Because of its adaptability, it is a useful tool in a variety of development contexts.

Maintaining Design Coherence:

Visual Copilot contributes to the preservation of design consistency among projects by automating the code generation process. It guarantees that design elements, such font, color, and spacing, are appropriately mirrored in the code. This uniformity promotes a unified digital identity by adhering to brand requirements and improving user experience.

Cooperation and Input:

Visual Copilot makes it easier for developers and designers to collaborate by giving the generated code a clear visual representation. Before work starts, teams can evaluate the code outputs and offer suggestions to improve the design. By using an iterative process, stakeholders can better align expectations and promote open communication.

Improving the Productivity of Developers:

Through the automation of tedious coding chores, Visual Copilot greatly increases developer productivity. Instead of wasting time on repetitive code creation, developers may concentrate on building more sophisticated functionality and features. This move not only accelerates the production timeframe but also encourages developers to engage in more innovative problem-solving.

5.2 UIZARD: AI FOR DEVELOPERS AND UX/UI DESIGNERS

Emerging as a revolutionary tool created especially for UI/UX designers and developers is Uizard. It expedites the design-to-development process by turning wireframes and mockups into usable frontend code.

Converting Concepts into Code:

With Uizard, designers can quickly sketch out their concepts using basic wireframes, which the program subsequently turns into working prototypes. This feature is especially helpful for rapid prototyping, as it allows teams to swiftly and effectively iterate on concepts. Uizard does a good job at bridging the gap between early design thoughts and the creation of a functional product.

Interface Friendly to Users:

Because of Uizard's user-friendly interface, designers with different levels of technical expertise can readily make use of its capabilities. The tool's drag-and-drop capability makes design creation easier and frees users to concentrate on creativity rather than intricate code. A wider audience may now access the design process thanks to this user-centric approach, which democratizes it.

Automated Generation of Frontend Code:

Following the creation of a design, Uizard uses AI algorithms to produce clear, responsive frontend code. The tool is compatible with major development environments because it supports a number of frameworks and libraries. This automated creation reduces the need for manual coding, minimizing the possibility of human errors and accelerating the development process.

Review of Iterative Design:

Because Uizard makes it simple to make changes and iterations, it facilitates successful collaboration between designers and developers. Changes to the wireframes can be made in response to input, and the tool will automatically update the relevant code. Because of this flexibility, a culture of continual development is promoted, guaranteeing that the finished product closely complies with consumer expectations.

Workflow Integration with Development:

The generated code from Uizard can be easily integrated

with current development workflows and given to developers in formats that operate with their favorite tools. The integration of Uizard into the development pipeline is guaranteed by this compatibility, which improves communication between the design and development teams.

5.3 TELEPORTHQ: DESIGN PROTOTYPES TO LIVE CODE

Leading the way in design-to-code technology is TeleportHQ, which provides developers with a stable platform to translate design prototypes into code that is ready for production. Teams can efficiently move from design to development because of its advantages.

Quick Testing and Prototyping:

TeleportHQ empowers designers to create interactive prototypes that can be tested with users before development begins. This feature allows teams to obtain valuable feedback early in the process, decreasing the chance of costly modifications later on. TeleportHQ improves the user experience and overall design quality by enabling quick prototyping.

Generating Live Code:

The most notable aspect of TeleportHQ is its capacity to produce live code straight from design concepts. By ensuring that the code appropriately matches the design, this feature helps to minimize differences between the two. In addition to accelerating development, live code generation frees up developers' time to concentrate on functionality rather than laboriously copying designs by hand.

Multiple Framework Support:

Like Visual Copilot, TeleportHQ is compatible with many frameworks, so developers may write code for popular environments like React and Vue. This flexibility allows teams to select the framework that best meets their project demands while benefiting from a streamlined design-to-code approach.

Reusability and Consistency in Design:

Teams may construct reusable components with TeleportHQ, which encourages design consistency. Teams may maintain a consistent look and feel across projects by creating a library of components that can be utilized for different projects. Developer workload is decreased and development speed is increased by this reusability.

Cooperation and Version Management:

TeleportHQ facilitates collaboration among team members by allowing many users to work on the same project simultaneously. Version management tools on the platform allow teams to keep track of changes and roll back to earlier versions as needed. By ensuring team alignment, this collaborative method improves the overall project workflow.

Design-to-code AI solutions such as TeleportHQ, Uizard, and Visual Copilot are completely changing the way developers and designers collaborate. These solutions assure design consistency, increase efficiency, and promote teamwork by automating the process of translating design into code. Using these design-to-code AI solutions will be essential for teams trying to produce high-quality products on schedule, as the digital world continues to change.

CHAPTER 6

AI Coding Tools for Collaboration

The use of AI-powered technologies improves communication and teamwork as software development becomes a more collaborative process. Developers may collaborate in real-time, document debates, and share information with one other thanks to collaborative AI coding tools, which promote a more effective and coordinated development process. We will look at three prominent tools in this field in this chapter: Replit Ghostwriter, Otter.ai, and Pieces for Developers. Each of these tools facilitates communication and streamlines workflows while addressing specific difficulties that development teams encounter.

6.1 Developer-Specific Parts: Enhanced Snippet Exchange

A cutting-edge technology called Pieces for Developers is

transforming the way development teams reuse, tag, and distribute code snippets. Pieces makes code more efficient and well-organized by utilizing AI technologies.

Intelligent Code Snippet Management: With Pieces, developers can easily generate, organize, and distribute code snippets. The platform analyzes snippets using artificial intelligence (AI) and tags them automatically based on usage patterns, functionality, and context. When looking for reusable code, developers can find relevant snippets more quickly thanks to this tagging system, which also saves them a lot of time.

Centralized Repository for Team Collaboration:
The application serves as a central location for team members to keep their snippets of code. Pieces promote cooperation among development teams by cultivating a culture of knowledge exchange. Because it's easy for team members to view each other's snippets, code reuse and best practices are encouraged across projects.

Informational Suggestions:
Pieces uses AI algorithms to provide developers with

contextual recommendations while they are coding. The program cuts down on the amount of time developers spend looking for answers by suggesting pertinent snippets as they type, based on the current project context. This feature not only increases output but also aids in preserving consistency of code across the project.

Integration with Development Environments: Developers may access Pieces' snippet library right from their coding environment thanks to Pieces' seamless integration with common IDEs. Because of this connectivity, the workflow is streamlined and developers may enter snippets without breaking their coding rhythm.

Snippet Version Control:
Version control is supported by the platform, which enables teams to monitor snippet modifications over time. By having access to the change history, developers can make sure they are always working with the most recent and pertinent code. This feature improves teamwork and reduces the possibility of adding erroneous or outdated code to projects.

6.2 OTTER.AI: DEVELOPMENT TEAMS' AI-POWERED TRANSCRIPTION

In software development, efficient communication is essential, particularly for code reviews and team meetings. By providing AI-powered transcribing services that guarantee accessibility and clarity in team discussions, Otter.ai offers a solution.

Reliable Transcripts for Code Evaluations:

Otter.ai creates precise transcriptions of meetings and conversations in real time using cutting edge speech recognition technology. Development teams may easily record brainstorming sessions, code reviews, and project updates with this feature. The transcripts that are produced are an invaluable tool for team members who were unable to attend the meeting or who need to review particular conversations.

Searchable Archives of Meetings:

The capability of Otter.ai to generate searchable transcription archives is one of its most notable capabilities. Team members don't need to go through long recordings to get important information because they can rapidly search for keywords or phrases in previous sessions. This feature makes critical ideas easily accessible and improves knowledge retention.

Integration with Collaboration Tools: Teams may simply record and transcribe meetings held on well-known collaboration platforms like Zoom, Microsoft Teams, and Google Meet thanks to Otter.ai's integration with these platforms. Teams may concentrate on talks without having to worry about taking manual notes thanks to this connection, which expedites the documentation process.

Team Member Collaboration Features:

By immediately adding comments, highlights, and action items to the transcriptions, team members can work together within Otter.ai. This interactive feature ensures that follow-up activities are assigned and properly described, while also encouraging participation during talks. Team members are able to uphold responsibility and transparency with regard to project duties as a consequence.

Considerations for Privacy and Security: Otter.ai places a high priority on user privacy and security, taking precautions to safeguard private information disclosed in meetings. Users can decide which transcriptions to share, so that only pertinent others are aware of important information. This functionality holds special significance for development teams engaged in delicate projects.

6.3 REPLIT GHOSTWRITER: AI-POWERED REAL-TIME COORDINATION

Replit Ghostwriter is a cutting-edge solution that uses AI ideas in real-time to improve group coding sessions. Regardless of where they are physically located, developers may collaborate efficiently thanks to this platform.

A dynamic coding environment

Replit Ghostwriter is a collaborative coding environment that enables numerous developers to work on projects at once. The application promotes teamwork and synergy among team members by letting users view modifications made by their peers in real time.

Code Suggestions Powered by AI:

As developers type code, Ghostwriter gives intelligent suggestions depending on the context of the project. The AI makes pertinent suggestions by examining the current codebase, which aids engineers in writing code more quickly. This function helps in knowledge transfer and skill development, which is especially advantageous for new team members or those who are not familiar with certain coding languages.

Combined Chat and Interaction Instruments:

Team members can communicate directly within Replit Ghostwriter thanks to its integrated chat feature. By doing away with the requirement for third-party communication platforms, this feature facilitates cooperation without interfering with the development process. In real time, developers may answer queries, talk about modifications to the code, and give comments.

Multiple Language Support:

Ghostwriter is adaptable for groups working on a variety of projects because it supports a large number of programming languages. The AI suggestions are optimized to match the requirements of each language, so developers working with Python, JavaScript, or any other language can enjoy a better coding experience.

Version Control and Project Management:

Version control tools included into the platform enable teams to monitor changes made to the codebase over time. Developers may monitor the history of revisions, collaborate on multiple branches, and rollback to previous versions if necessary. This degree of project management makes certain that groups keep a clear picture of their workload and encourages team members to take responsibility for their actions.

Collaborative AI coding tools like Replit Ghostwriter, Otter.ai, and Pieces for Developers are changing the software development industry. These tools help development teams work more productively and efficiently by promoting real-time collaboration, boosting snippet sharing, and boosting communication. Using these collaborative AI solutions will be crucial for teams trying to produce high-quality work while keeping a flexible and responsive workflow as the software development industry develops.

CHAPTER 7

AI Tools for Particular Programming Languages

Developers are finding customized AI tools for particular programming languages to be quite helpful in the ever-changing field of software development. By streamlining the coding process, increasing productivity, and lowering errors, these technologies free up engineers to concentrate more on addressing complicated issues than handling tedious chores. This chapter explores AI tools made especially for Python, JavaScript, TypeScript, Swift, and Kotlin, emphasizing their special qualities and advantages.

7.1 Python Developers' AI Tools

Python's ease of use and adaptability have made it one of the most widely used computer languages. A number of AI tools have been created especially for Python developers to improve the development process even more.

Kite:

With Kite, a top AI-powered coding helper, Python coders can create code more quickly and effectively. It has a number of features:

1. **Completion of Code:** Kite greatly accelerates the development process by using machine learning methods to deliver intelligent code completions as developers type.

2. **Documentation on Function:** Kite displays appropriate documentation for functions and libraries right in the code editor, eliminating the need for developers to switch contexts and hunt for information online.

3. **Complete Lines of Code:** This feature streamlines the coding process by allowing developers to finish full lines of code with a single keystroke.

PyCharm AI: JetBrains' A robust Integrated Development Environment (IDE) designed specifically for Python development is PyCharm. The capabilities of AI are improved with the addition of features:

1. **Smart Code Analysis:** PyCharm AI scans code for

any errors and makes recommendations for corrections. It uses static code analysis to find problems before they arise, assisting developers in finding mistakes as soon as possible.

2. **Refactoring recommendations:** With the help of the IDE's intelligent refactoring recommendations, developers may efficiently reorganize their code without creating new defects.

3. **Machine Learning Library Integration:** The smooth interface that PyCharm AI provides with well-known machine learning libraries like TensorFlow and PyTorch facilitates the incorporation of AI models into applications by developers.

Bug identification and Testing: The Python ecosystem's AI-powered tools can automate testing and bug identification, cutting down on the amount of time needed for manual testing. These technologies ensure a more robust end product by analyzing code coverage and offering insights regarding untested sections.

7.2 AI ASSISTANTS FOR JAVASCRIPT AND TYPESCRIPT

The basic languages for web development are JavaScript and TypeScript. While TypeScript offers type safety for bigger systems, JavaScript is necessary for frontend development. Code quality and developer efficiency are increased by AI technologies designed specifically for these languages.

Tabnine:

The AI-powered code completion tool Tabnine works with a number of well-known editors and IDEs. It offers the following advantages to TypeScript and JavaScript developers:

1. **Contextual Code Suggestions:** Tabnine examines current code to offer completions that are sensitive to the particular coding conventions and styles employed in a project.

2. **Group Education:** With time, Tabnine gains knowledge from a team's codebase and refines its recommendations according to the particular procedures and standards followed by the group. This is particularly useful in cooperative settings.

Now a part of Snyk, DeepCode:

DeepCode is an AI-driven code review tool designed to find flaws and problems with the quality of code in JavaScript and TypeScript applications.

1. **Instant Commentary:** DeepCode helps developers follow best practices by analyzing code in real time and offering recommendations to improve code quality.

2. **Identifying Security Vulnerabilities:** The tool ensures that programs are secure in addition to being functional by identifying potential security issues in the code.

CodeSandbox:

An online code editor called CodeSandbox makes it easier to collaborate and prototype quickly when writing JavaScript and TypeScript code.

1. **Features for Live Collaboration:** The technology enables real-time AI features to offer changes and code snippets to developers working on the same codebase at the same time.

2. **Ready-made Designs:** With CodeSandbox,

developers can rapidly get started on projects by accessing templates for popular frameworks and libraries.

7.3 USING KOTLIN AND SWIFT FOR AI IN MOBILE DEVELOPMENT

Swift and Kotlin-based mobile development for iOS and Android has become very popular. AI tools designed specifically for these languages improve and streamline the development process.

1. **SwiftLint and SwiftFormat:** By enforcing coding standards and stylistic rules, these tools improve the quality of code in Swift development.
2. **Code Linting:** SwiftLint helps developers maintain a clean codebase by analyzing code for possible problems and enforcing recommended practices.
3. **Automatic Formatting:** SwiftFormat ensures consistency across the project by automatically formatting code in accordance with specified style requirements.

IntelliJ IDEA Kotlin Plugin:

JetBrains' IntelliJ IDEA provides strong support for Kotlin development. The features of AI comprise:

1. **Smart Code Completion:** The IDE delivers intelligent code suggestions, making it easier for developers to write Kotlin code fast and accurately.

2. **Refactoring Assistance:** Intelligent refactoring tools in the IDE enable developers to securely rearrange code without sacrificing functionality.

3. **Static Code Analysis:** IntelliJ IDEA analyzes Kotlin code for potential mistakes, delivering real-time suggestions for improvement and minimizing the risk of defects.

Firebase:

1. **Firebase ML Kit:** This tool provides machine learning capabilities that may be incorporated into mobile applications for Swift and Kotlin mobile developers.

2. **Device-Level ML:** By implementing machine learning models that operate directly on mobile devices, the kit enables developers to enhance user experience and performance.

3. **Ready-made Models:** Firebase lets developers add sophisticated features without needing a lot of experience with machine learning because it offers pre-trained models for common tasks like word recognition and image identification.

Developers of Python, JavaScript, TypeScript, Swift, and Kotlin greatly benefit from AI tools designed for particular programming languages. These technologies enable developers to concentrate on coming up with creative solutions and producing high-caliber apps by automating monotonous activities, optimizing code quality, and simplifying code completion. Software development will be significantly shaped by the use of AI technologies as the technology landscape continues to change.

CHAPTER 8

AI Tools Integrated into IDEs

The foundation of software development are integrated development environments (IDEs), which give programmers the resources they need to efficiently write, test, and debug code. Artificial intelligence has led to the inclusion of AI-driven capabilities in many IDEs that greatly improve the programming experience. The top IDEs with AI tools integrated are examined in this chapter, with an emphasis on their special features and the ways they are revolutionizing development practices.

8.1 AI-Centric Development Environment: Cursor IDE

A new generation of development environments with AI integration at their core is embodied by Cursor IDE. Cursor was created from the bottom up with the goal of increasing coding productivity through intelligent support. Here are a few of its noteworthy attributes:

Suggested Intelligent Code:

With the use of sophisticated machine learning techniques, Cursor offers context-aware code recommendations that enable developers to efficiently finish lines of code or entire functions. The recommendations are made with the particular coding styles and patterns that are used in the project in mind.

Generation of Code:

Cursor's ability to automatically produce boilerplate code is one of its best capabilities. By doing this, developers may spend much less time on tedious activities and more time on more intricate logic and features.

Intelligent Coordination:

Cursor enables team members to collaborate in real time and allows multiple developers to work together on the same codebase. The AI expedites the collaborative process by helping to reconcile modifications and settle disputes.

Integrated Debugging Features:

The IDE features AI-powered debugging tools that evaluate code in real time, delivering fast feedback on any flaws. This proactive method to debugging lets engineers find and handle mistakes before they worsen.

Adaptable AI Frameworks:

Within Cursor, developers may train custom AI models to fit their unique development methods and workflows. This flexibility guarantees that the AI becomes a crucial component of the developer's arsenal, customized to meet their specific requirements.

Cursor IDE is a prime example of how artificial intelligence (AI) may transform the software development industry by offering tools that boost efficiency while simultaneously enhancing code quality and teamwork.

8.2 AI CODING VISUAL STUDIO CODE EXTENSIONS

Developers like Visual Studio Code (VS Code), a very popular and flexible code editor, because of its versatility. There are a ton of AI-powered extensions available that greatly improve the entire programming experience. An overview of a few well-known AI VS Code extensions is provided below:

Copilot for GitHub:

As developers type, this addon provides context-aware code suggestions that blend in smoothly with VS Code. Based on comments and existing code, GitHub Copilot uses OpenAI's Codex model to deliver intelligent completions, suggesting complete functions or even sophisticated algorithms.

Tabnine:

Deep learning is used by Tabnine to provide code completions for a variety of languages. Because it can learn from the developer's codebase, it can make customized recommendations that fit the project's needs and particular coding style.

Kite:

Kite seamlessly incorporates code documentation and AI-powered completions into the VS Code environment. Developers can more easily implement new methods without having to look for external documentation because of its line-of-code completions, quick documentation, and example functionality.

CodeGPT:

CodeGPT uses natural language prompts to generate code snippets, leveraging OpenAI's GPT models to help developers. This can be very helpful for engineers who want to comprehend complex algorithms or quickly prototype concepts.

Linting Tools Powered by AI:

AI capabilities can also be incorporated by extensions like ESLint and Prettier to offer more intelligent formatting and linting recommendations. These tools examine code for style and quality, recommending fixes that match with best practices.

These add-ons demonstrate how artificial intelligence (AI) may be used to improve Visual Studio Code, giving programmers the means to produce better organized, effective code while lessening the mental strain that comes with it.

8.3 AI-Capable JetBrains IDEs

Known for its powerful suite of integrated development environments (IDEs), JetBrains has integrated AI-driven capabilities into its popular IDEs, WebStorm, PyCharm, and IntelliJ IDEA, to improve developer productivity. The following are some noteworthy AI features of JetBrains IDEs:

Clever Finish:

The Smart Completion feature in JetBrains IDEs makes code recommendations depending on the current context. Based on the surrounding code, our intelligent suggestion system predicts which candidates are most likely to be completed, which aids developers.

Code Reviews and Recommendations:

The IDEs use sophisticated static code analysis to instantly spot possible problems. The project's unique language and framework-specific best practices and refactoring possibilities are among the contextual recommendations for code enhancements that developers receive.

Refactoring Powered by AI:

With AI support, JetBrains IDEs expedite the refactoring process and enable developers to safely reorganize code. To ensure that modifications don't result in the introduction of new problems or faults, the AI examines dependencies and possible side effects.

Integrated Machine Learning:

JetBrains IDEs give developers working with machine learning models the tools they need to easily incorporate AI libraries. This includes debugging and creating machine learning applications more efficiently thanks to support for well-known frameworks like PyTorch and TensorFlow.

Integrated Version Control System:

The integrated version control tools in JetBrains IDEs improve teamwork and project management by leveraging artificial intelligence (AI) to recommend branch management tactics and code merging choices.

By integrating AI capabilities into their IDEs, JetBrains increases the developer experience, making it easier to write high-quality code efficiently while lowering the overhead associated with manual code management activities.

The integration of AI tools within integrated programming environments (IDEs) as Cursor, Visual Studio Code, and JetBrains IDEs signifies a noteworthy progress in the field of software development. These AI-powered capabilities increase code quality and developer cooperation in addition to increasing coding productivity. Programming will likely become more and more shaped by AI technology's incorporation into development environments as it develops, freeing developers to concentrate on originality and creativity rather than repetitive duties.

CHAPTER 9

ROBOTICS-BASED CODE MAINTENANCE TOOLS

Effective project management and maintaining code quality are crucial components of the software development lifecycle. AI solutions for code maintenance are essential for enhancing teamwork, automating time-consuming operations, and maintaining the health of codebases over time. This chapter explores the essential AI tools and techniques for code maintenance, with a particular emphasis on automated bug finding and repair, version control integration, and the creation of unit tests.

9.1 AUTOMATED BUG FINDING AND CORRECTION

AI algorithms are used by automated bug identification and repair programs to find possible flaws in codebases before they become serious ones. These tools allow for real-time feedback and fixes by analyzing code as developers create it.

DeepCode:

DeepCode is an AI-powered application that uses cutting-edge machine learning algorithms to search codebases for vulnerabilities and defects. It leverages expertise gleaned from a sizable repository of open-source projects and analyzes code patterns. The following are some salient characteristics:

- **In-the-Moment Analysis:** DeepCode gives programmers immediate feedback on possible problems like logical fallacies, performance snags, and security flaws as they write code. This proactive strategy aids in the early detection of bugs during the development process.

- **Program Suggestions:** In addition to identifying issues, DeepCode provides best-practice-based repair recommendations. For example, it can recommend different code styles or libraries that enhance speed and security.

- **Using IDEs for Integration:** Because DeepCode easily interacts with well-known IDEs, developers may easily add bug detection to their current workflows. With the help of this connection, developers may get real-time feedback without having to stop working on their code.

Additional AI Bug Detection Resources:

AI-driven techniques are also used by tools like as Snyk and CodeQL to scan codebases for vulnerabilities. These platforms concentrate on locating acknowledged security flaws and giving developers useful information for fixing them.

In addition to improving code quality, automated bug detection technologies relieve engineers of the laborious chore of manual debugging, freeing them up to concentrate on more strategic work.

9.2 AI SUPPORT AND VERSION CONTROL

In today's software development world, version control

systems (VCS) such as GitHub and GitLab are essential for effective teamwork and code change management. These systems' capabilities are increased and excellent code quality is maintained when AI tools are integrated with them.

Commit Analysis Driven by AI:

Certain AI systems examine commit histories in order to identify trends in coding practices. These tools can:

- **Provide Feedback:** Depending on the complexity of changes, AI can recommend improved commit messages, promote more frequent commits, or point out the need for more code reviews.

- **Assess Code Problems:** AI can identify parts of the codebase that might become troublesome based on bugs or issues that have previously been reported in files that are comparable by examining historical commit data.

Automated Reviews of Code:

Code review processes can be partially automated by AI-driven technologies, which identify possible problems before human reviewers get involved. This comprises:

- **Style Checks:** Verifying that the code complies with the required style standards.
- **Logic Errors:** Recognizing typical logical fallacies and recommending fixes based on previously applied codebase updates.

Using CI/CD Pipelines for Integration:

Pipelines for Continuous Integration and Continuous Deployment (CI/CD) can be improved by AI tools via:

- **Testing Predictions:** Making use of past data to forecast which tests, in light of recent modifications, are most likely to fail in order to optimize the testing procedure.

- **Automated Merging:** To save developers time,

certain AI systems can evaluate pull requests and, if specific criteria are satisfied, automate the merging process.

Development teams may retain excellent code quality while improving productivity and communication by integrating AI with version control systems.

9.3 UNIT TEST DEVELOPMENT AND UPKEEP

Robust software development is based on thorough unit testing. Unit test creation and upkeep, however, can be labor-intensive. These days, AI technologies are intervening to speed up this procedure, lowering technical debt and raising the general caliber of the code.

Automated Test Generation:

Machine learning methods are used by AI-driven solutions such as Test.ai and Ponicode to evaluate code and produce unit tests automatically. Some of these tools' salient features are:

- **Contextual Understanding:** These tools build tests that cover a range of scenarios, including edge cases that developers might miss, by analyzing the logic of functions and methods.

- **Examining Coverage:** To make sure that all crucial paths in the codebase are sufficiently validated, AI may assess the test coverage that is currently in place and recommend areas that require additional testing.

Maintenance of Tests:

Writing and maintaining unit tests can be as difficult, particularly when there are changes to the code. AI tools are beneficial in the following ways:

- **Automated Updates for Tests:** AI tools can recognize which tests require updating when code is refactored and can make recommendations for changes automatically to keep the tests current and functional.

- **Failure Diagnosis:** AI may examine failed tests to

find recurring themes or problems, giving developers information that speeds up problem diagnosis.

Decrease in Technical Debt:

AI tools considerably lower the technical debt related to testing by automating the creation and upkeep of unit tests. Instead of wasting too much time writing and updating tests, developers may concentrate on developing new features.

Incorporating AI into the creation and upkeep of unit tests boosts developer productivity and increases software reliability, allowing teams to produce high-quality products more quickly.

AI-powered code maintenance technologies provide revolutionary advantages for a number of software development life cycle stages. These technologies assist in maintaining high code quality and lessening the workload associated with manual operations. They range from automated bug detection and fixing to improved version control integration and intelligent unit test development.

Development teams may maintain the strength and efficiency of their codebases and ultimately produce software projects that are more successful by utilizing AI-driven solutions.

CHAPTER 10

AI-ASSISTED CODING'S FUTURE

The use of artificial intelligence (AI) in software development is changing how developers approach coding tasks as a result of the rapid advancement of technology. With an emphasis on specialized AI agents, the optimization of CI/CD pipelines, and the ethical issues surrounding AI's involvement in software development, this chapter explores the exciting future of AI-assisted coding.

10.1 DEVELOPERS' USE OF CUSTOMIZED AI AGENTS

The way developers can use AI in their processes has significantly advanced with the introduction of micro AI agents. These agents improve the development process overall by concentrating on particular coding tasks, such as testing, debugging, and optimization.

Features Particular to Tasks:

Specialized AI agents focus on certain areas of development, whereas generic AI tools aim to handle a wide range of coding activities. This enables them to provide help that is more focused and efficient. Among the crucial roles are:

1. **Installing Agents:** These agents find and fix mistakes in code by analyzing it. They can provide recommendations for fixes based on historical data and typical coding errors by using lessons learned from past debugging sessions.

2. **Agents for Testing:** AI testing agents may generate test cases automatically, guaranteeing thorough coverage of all code functionalities. They can minimize manual labor by adjusting tests in response to code modifications.

3. **Agents of Optimization:** These agents, which concentrate on code efficiency, can evaluate algorithms and recommend enhancements for scalability, memory utilization, and performance. They might even offer advice on best practices based on the most recent developments in software development.

Integrated Effortlessly with Development Tools:

Developers may readily access specialized AI agents by integrating them into their current development environments (IDEs) and processes. With real-time help and feedback enabled by this integration, productivity is increased without interfering with the development process.

Interaction Between AI Agents:

Yet another intriguing breakthrough is the possibility of cooperation amongst specialist AI bots. Together, these agents can take on difficult coding problems that could call for a diversified approach, resulting in more efficient fixes and better overall code quality.

The emergence of specialized AI agents represents a move toward more focused and effective coding techniques, freeing up developers to concentrate on higher-level work while reaping the benefits of automated assistance for specialized and repetitive activities.

10.2 AI's PLACE IN CONTINUOUS DEPLOYMENT AND INTEGRATION (CI/CD)

Modern software development requires the use of continuous integration and deployment, or CI/CD, which enables teams to produce high-quality software more regularly and consistently. AI is playing an increasingly crucial role in streamlining CI/CD pipelines, automating numerous activities and raising overall efficiency.

Deployment Task Automation:

The amount of manual labor needed to deliver code updates to production environments can be decreased by using AI technology to automate deployment operations. Important elements consist of:

1. **Smart Deployment:** By weighing variables like system load, user activity, and possible dangers, AI can evaluate the effects of changes and determine when to deploy.

2. **Reversible Systems:** In case of deployment errors, AI can automatically start rollback operations based on established criteria, minimizing downtime and ensuring system stability.

Improved Automation of Testing:

A crucial part of CI/CD is testing, and AI greatly improves this stage by:

1. **Predictive Analysis:** AI algorithms can forecast which areas of the code are most likely to break based on previous data, directing testing efforts where they are required most. This aids in testing phase resource allocation optimization.

2. **Automatic Testing for Regression:** Regression testing can be automated using AI, preventing errors from being introduced into previously functional features by fresh code changes. AI can increase test execution speed and accuracy by continuously learning from previous test results.

Intelligent Tracking and Input:

After deployment, AI tools can offer real-time application performance monitoring. They immediately detect any problems by analyzing system metrics and user interactions. This feedback loop helps developers to:

1. **Proactively Address Issues:** Teams may handle performance snags or user experience problems

before they worsen by using the insights that artificial intelligence provides.

2. **Ongoing Enhancement:** Teams can gain insights into application performance and user behavior over time with the use of AI-driven analytics, which can then be used to shape future deployment and development plans.

Organizations may achieve faster and more dependable software delivery, which will eventually increase customer happiness and propel corporate success, by utilizing AI in CI/CD pipelines.

10.3 SOFTWARE DEVELOPMENT'S ETHICAL AI CONSIDERATIONS

Although there are many advantages to using AI-assisted coding in software development, there are also some ethical issues to be aware of. These worries center on the loss of jobs, the use of machine-generated code, and the wider effects of AI in the creative industries.

Problems with Work Displacement:

As AI technologies automate many coding processes, there is a rising danger that they may displace human developers. Important things to think about are as follows:

1. **Changing Positions:** AI can open up new chances for developers to concentrate on higher-level tasks like system design, architecture, and AI tool management, even while some traditional coding professions may disappear. In this field, experts must be able to adapt.

2. **Needs for Upskilling:** In order to stay relevant, developers must embrace lifelong learning and acquire skills in sophisticated problem-solving, ethical programming, and AI management.

Utilization of Automated Code:

Concerns regarding quality, maintainability, and comprehension are brought up by the growing usage of AI-generated code:

1. **Assurance of Code Quality:** There is a concern that reliance on AI-generated code may lead to poor-quality code if developers do not fully understand the logic behind it. It is crucial to make sure that machine-generated code is thoroughly

reviewed and tested.

2. **Loss of Expertise:** An excessive dependence on AI technologies may cause developers' capacity for critical thought and problem-solving to deteriorate. It is essential to find a balance between using AI support and continuing to be proficient in coding.

Bias and Accountability: Prejudices that are present in the training data may inadvertently be reinforced by AI systems. This may give rise to moral dilemmas in coding procedures:

1. **Algorithm Biases:** Programming that is biased can be produced by AI systems trained on biased datasets, which could have an impact on functionality and user experience. The biases must be addressed proactively by developers and they must stay alert.

2. **Accountability for Decisions Made by AI:** Accountability issues surface as AI systems become increasingly self-sufficient in their decision-making. When using AI tools for coding, developers and organizations need to set explicit criteria for accountability.

Ensuring that AI improves software development without sacrificing quality, innovation, or fairness requires addressing these ethical issues. Having continuous conversations on the development implications of AI will assist to design a future in which technology enhances human skill rather than replaces it.

In conclusion, there is a bright future for AI-assisted coding, marked by customized AI agents that simplify development work, improved CI/CD procedures that make use of automation, and the constant requirement to take these developments' ethical implications into account. It will be essential for developers and organizations to negotiate these developments carefully and ethically as AI develops further in order to maximize advantages and minimize risks.

ABOUT THE AUTHOR

 Technology specialist and author Emma Royce Smartley specializes in the newest developments in AI, coding tools, and software development. His goal as a writer is to help developers and tech fans remain ahead of the curve by simplifying difficult tech ideas. His publications provide insightful analyses of how new technologies are changing the landscape of productivity and software development. Emma's love of innovation propels him to investigate and elucidate the technologies that will shape the landscape of the future.

www.ingramcontent.com/pod-product-compliance
Lightning Source LLC
LaVergne TN
LVHW051713050326
832903LV00032B/4178